Let's Bring Mom Breakfast

Learning the BR Sound

Sharon McConnell

Phonics
for the
REAL World™

Rosen Classroom Books and Materials™
New York

It is Mother's Day! Let's bring Mom breakfast.

3

I get the bread.

Dad breaks brown eggs in a pan and cooks them.

I bring Dad the milk.

Oops! I broke a glass.

I bring Dad the broom.

Dad cleans up the broken glass.

Mom's breakfast is ready.

17

We bring Mom's breakfast to her room.

19

Mom likes her breakfast!

Word List

bread

breakfast

breaks

bring

broke

broken

broom

brown

Instructional Guide

One of the essential skills that enable a young child to read is the ability to associate letter-sound symbols and blend these sounds to form words. Phonics instruction can teach children a system that will help them decode unfamiliar words and, in turn, enhance their word-recognition skills. We offer a phonics-based series of books that are easy to read and understand. Each book pairs words and pictures that reinforce specific phonetic sounds in a logical sequence. Topics are based on curriculum goals appropriate for early readers in the areas of science, social studies, and health.

Letters/Sound: **br** – Review color words *blue, black, brown.* Ask the child to tell which two have exactly the same beginning sound. Have them underline and name the **bl** or **br** sound in each word.

- Provide the child with a brown response card to hold up when they hear words beginning with **br.** Pronounce the following words: *breakfast, back, brush, brake, bring, broke, bean, brown, brick, brother, broom, black, breath, barn, bread,* etc. List **br** words as the child responds. Have them underline **br** in each of the words.
- Have the child name additional **br** words to add to the above list. Ask them to use the words in oral sentences.

Phonics Activities: Have the child name the **br** words they hear in sentences, such as the following: *The new brick house has brown doors. We will bring bread home from the store. Brad brags about his brother's winning baseball team. Mary broke her leg when she fell crossing the bridge. The light from the sun is very bright.* List the child's responses. Have them underline **br** in each word.

- Identify the word *bright* in the list from the previous activity. Have the child replace the initial **br** with a single consonant to form rhyming words: *light, might, night, right, sight, tight.* Help the child apply the same principle to other **br** words (*bring – sing, brown – town, brick – sick, brake – take*).
- Pose riddles about **br** words. (Example: *This is something good to eat. You bake it in the oven. It can be white or brown. You can use it to make a sandwich. What is it?*) List riddle answers and have the child underline the initial **br** sound in each of them.

Additional Resources:
- Arno, Iris H. *I Love You, Mom.* Mahwah, NJ: Troll Communications L.L.C., 1998.
- Black, Sonia W. *Hanging Out with Mom.* New York: Scholastic, Inc., 1997.
- Kaplan, John. *Mom & Me.* New York: Scholastic, Inc., 1997.
- Schaefer, Lola M. *Mothers.* Mankato, MN: Capstone Press, Inc., 1999.

Published in 2002 by The Rosen Publishing Group, Inc.
29 East 21st Street, New York, NY 10010

Book Design: Haley Wilson

Photo Credits: Karey Shuckers-Churley

McConnell, Sharon, 1971-
  Let's bring mom breakfast : learning the BR sound / Sharon McConnell.
    p. cm. — (Power phonics/phonics for the real world)
  ISBN 0-8239-5936-8 (library binding)
  ISBN 0-8239-8281-5 (pbk.)
  6-pack ISBN 0-8239-9249-7
  1. Breakfasts—Juvenile literature. 2. English language—
Consonants—Juvenile literature. [1. Breakfasts 2. English Language—
Consonants] I. Title. II. Series.
      2002
  641.5'2—dc21

Manufactured in the United States of America